Sacred Reflections

A Visual Walk through Scripture

Verses from King James Bible
Photography by: Connie Henry

TRILOGY
A wholly owned subsidiary of TBN

Trilogy Christian Publishers
A Wholly Owned Subsidary of Trinity Broadcasting Network
2442 Michelle Drive
Tustin, CA 92780

Sacred Reflections: A Visual Walk through Scripture

For information, address Trilogy Christian Publishing
Rights Department, 2442 Michelle Drive, Tustin, CA 92780.

Trilogy Christian Publishing/ TBN and colophon are trademarks of Trinity Broadcasting Network.

For information about special discounts for bulk purchases, please contact Trilogy Christian Publishing.

Trilogy Disclaimer: The views and content expressed in this book are those of the author and may not necessarily reflect the views and doctrine of Trilogy Christian Publishing or the Trinity Broadcasting Network.

10 9 8 7 6 5 4 3 2 1

Library of Congress Cataloging-in-Publication Data is available.

ISBN 979-8-89333-996-3

ISBN 979-8-89333-997-0 (ebook)

Genesis

In the beginning, God created the heavens and the earth.
Genesis 1:1

And God said,
Let there be light:
and there was light.
Genesis 1:3

So God created man in His own image, in the image of God created He him; male and female created He them.
Genesis 1:27

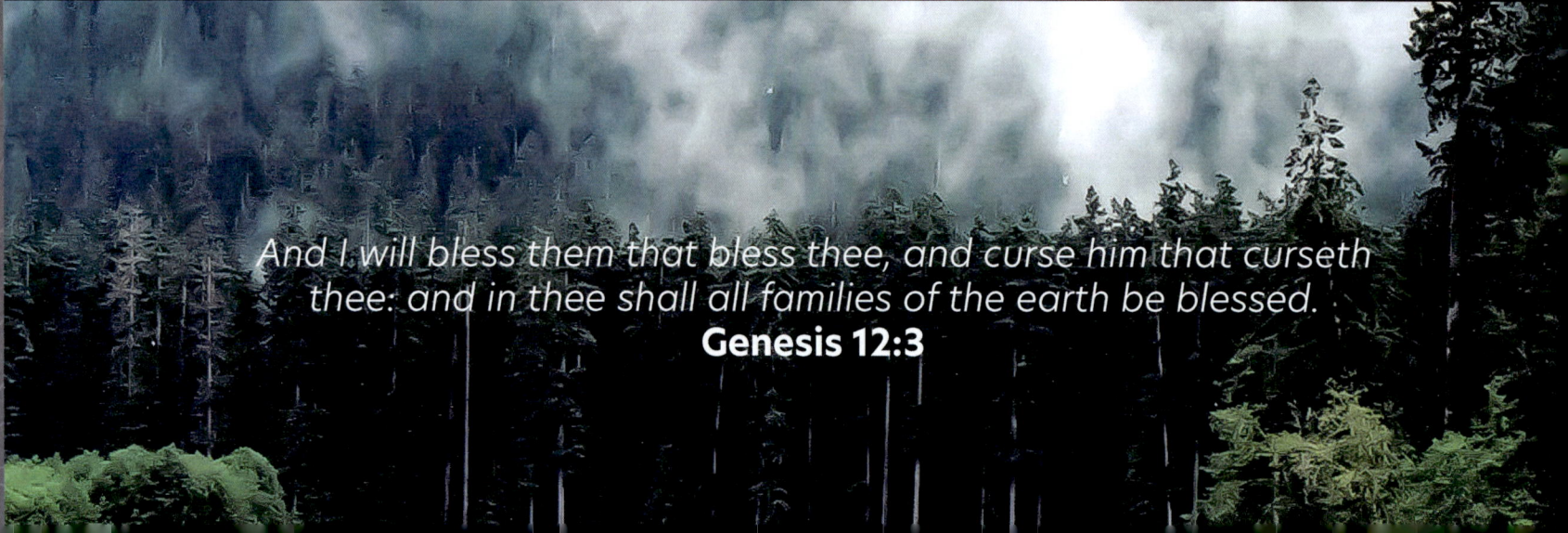

And I will bless them that bless thee, and curse him that curseth thee: and in thee shall all families of the earth be blessed.
Genesis 12:3

But lift up thy rod, and stretch out thy hand over the sea, and divide it: and the children of Israel shall go on dry ground through the midst of the sea
Exodus 14:16

Exodus

Thou in Thy mercy hast led forth the people which thou hast redeemed: thou hast guided them in Thy strength unto Thy holy habitation.
Exodus 15:13

Leviticus

For the life of the flesh is in the blood: and I have given it to you upon the altar to make an atonement for your souls: for it is the blood that maketh an atonement for the soul.
Leviticus 17:11

Thou shalt not avenge, nor bear any grudge against the children of thy people, but thou shalt love thy neighbour as thyself: I am the LORD.
Leviticus 19:18

Numbers

The LORD make his face shine upon thee, and be gracious unto thee
Numbers 6:25

Deuteronomy

The LORD God of your fathers make you a thousand times so many more as ye are, and bless you, as he hath promised you!
Deuteronomy 1:11

He is thy praise, and he is thy God, that hath done for thee hese great and terrible things, which thine eyes have seen.
Deuteronomy 10:21

Unto thee it was shewed, that thou mightest know that the LORD he is God; there is none else beside him.
Deuteronomy 4:35

Joshua

And if it seem evil unto you to serve the LORD , choose you this day whom ye will serve; whether the gods which your fathers served that were on the other side of the flood, or the gods of the Amorites, in whose land ye dwell: **but as for me and my house, we will serve the LORD.**
Joshua 24:15

Judges

And the angel of the LORD appeared unto him, and said unto him, The LORD is with thee, thou mighty man of valour.
Judges 6:12

Ruth

And Ruth said, Intreat me not to leave thee, or to return from following after thee: for whither thou goest, I will go; and where thou lodgest, I will lodge: thy people shall be my people, and thy God my God: where thou diest, will I die, and there will I be buried: the LORD do so to me, and more also, if ought but death part thee and me.
Ruth 1:16-17

1 & 2 Samuel

Only fear the LORD , and serve him in truth with all your heart: for consider how great things he hath done for you.
1 Samuel 12:24

For all his judgments were before me: And as for his statutes, I did not depart from them.
2 Samuel 22:23

Hear me, O LORD,
me, that this peopl
may know that tho
art the LORD God,
that thou hast turn
their heart back ag
1 Kings 18:37

Notwithstanding they would not hear, but hardened their necks, like to the neck of their fathers, that did not believe in the LORD their God. And they rejected his statutes, and his covenant that he made with their fathers, and his testimonies which he testified against them; and they followed vanity, and became vain, and went after the heathen that were round about them, concerning whom the LORD had charged them, that they should not do like them. And they left all the commandments of the LORD their God, and made them molten images, even two calves, and made a grove, and worshipped all the host of heaven, and served Baal.

2 Kings 17:14-16

1 & 2 Kings

Now therefore, O LORD our God, I beseech thee, save thou us out of his hand, that all the kingdoms of the earth may know that thou art the LORD God, even thou only.

2 Kings 19:19

1 Chronicles

O give thanks unto the LORD; for he is good; For his mercy endureth for ever.
1 Chronicles 16:34

Be ye strong therefore, and let not your hands be weak: for your work shall be rewarded.

2 Chronicles 15:7

2 Chronicles

Ezra

And they sang together by course in praising and giving thanks unto the LORD ; because he is good, for his mercy endureth for ever toward Israel. And all the people shouted with a great shout, when they praised the LORD , because the foundation of the house of the LORD was laid.
Ezra 3:11

Nehemiah

But if ye turn unto me, and keep my commandments, and do them; though there were of you cast out unto the uttermost part of the heaven, yet will I gather them from thence, and will bring them unto the place that I have chosen to set my name there.
Nehemiah 1:9

Esther

For if thou altogether holdest thy peace at this time, then shall there enlargement and deliverance arise to the Jews from another place; but thou and thy father's house shall be destroyed: and who knoweth whether thou art come to the kingdom for such a time as this?
Esther 4:14

Thou hast granted me life and favour, And thy visitation hath preserved my spirit.
Job 10:12

In whose hand is the soul of every living thing, And the breath of all mankind.
Job 12:10

Though he slay me, yet will I trust in him: But I will maintain mine own ways before him.
Job 13:15

For I know that my redeemer liveth, And that he shall stand at the latter day upon the earth:
Job 19:25

Job

Psalms

Blessed is the man that walketh not in the counsel of the ungodly, nor standeth in the way of sinners, Nor sitteth in the seat of the scornful.

Psalm 1:1

I will praise thee, O LORD, with my whole heart; I will shew forth all thy marvellous works.
Psalm 9:1

———

The fool hath said in his heart, there is no God. They are corrupt, they have done abominable works, There is none that doeth good.
Psalm 14:1

The heavens declare the glory of God; And the firmament sheweth his handywork.
Psalm 19:1

Proverbs

The fear of the LORD is the beginning of knowledge: But fools despise wisdom and instruction.
Proverbs 1:7

The fear of the LORD is the beginning of wisdom: And the knowledge of the holy is understanding.
Proverbs 9:10

Trust in the LORD with all thine heart; And lean not unto thine own understanding.
Proverbs 3:5

For in much wisdom is much grief: and he that increaseth knowledge increaseth sorrow.
Ecclesiastes 1:18

Then shall the dust return to the earth as it was: and the spirit shall return unto God who gave it.
Ecclesiastes 12:7

Let us hear the conclusion of the whole matter: Fear God, and keep his commandments: for this is the whole duty of man.
Ecclesiastes 12:13

Ecclesiastes

Song of Solomon

The flowers appear on the earth; The time of the singing of birds is come, And the voice of the turtle Is heard in our land;
Song of Solomon 2:12

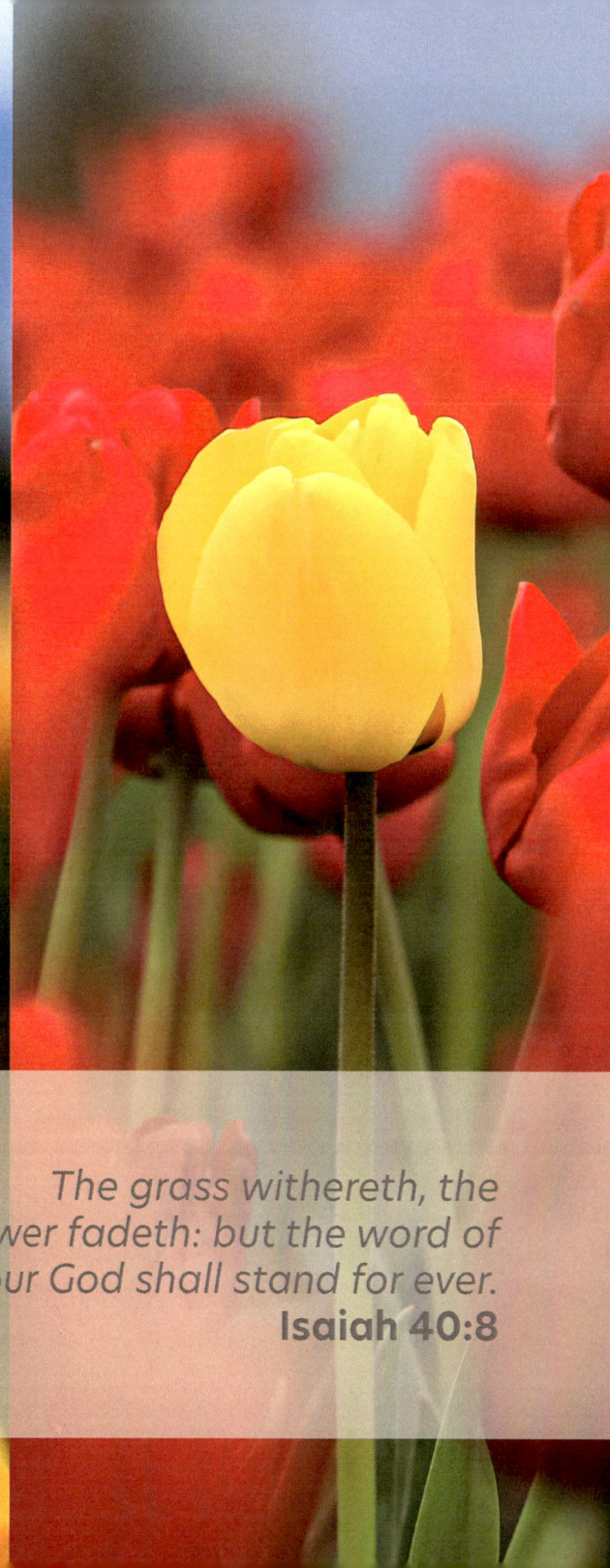

The grass withereth, the flower fadeth: but the word of our God shall stand for ever.

Isaiah 40:8

Isaiah

Jeremiah

And ye shall be my people, and I will be your God.
Jeremiah 30:22

Lamentations

The LORD is good unto them that wait for him, To the soul that seeketh him.
Lamentations 3:25

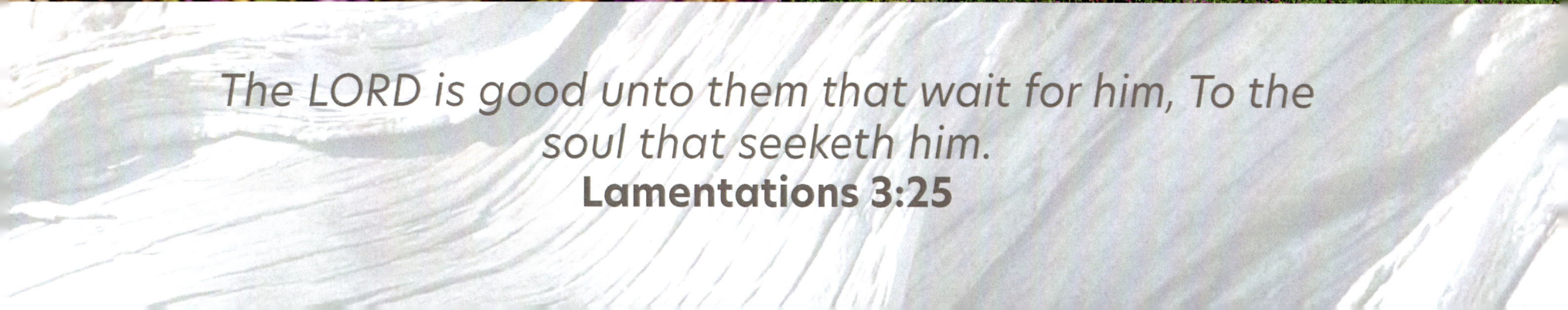

Ezekiel

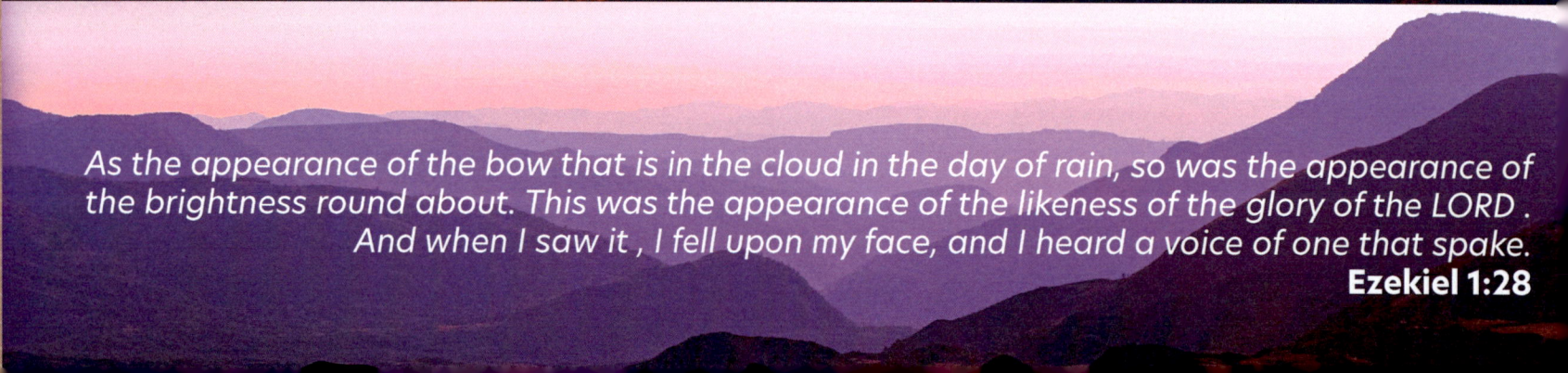

As the appearance of the bow that is in the cloud in the day of rain, so was the appearance of the brightness round about. This was the appearance of the likeness of the glory of the LORD . And when I saw it , I fell upon my face, and I heard a voice of one that spake.

Ezekiel 1:28

And at that time shall Michael stand up, the great prince which standeth for the children of thy people: and there shall be a time of trouble, such as never was since there was a nation even to that same time: and at that time thy people shall be delivered, every one that shall be found written in the book. And many of them that sleep in the dust of the earth shall awake, some to everlasting life, and some to shame and everlasting contempt. And they that be wise shall shine as the brightness of the firmament; and they that turn many to righteousness as the stars for ever and ever.

Daniel 12:1-3

Daniel

Hosea

Sow to yourselves in righteousness, reap in mercy; break up your fallow ground: for it is time to seek the LORD, till he come and rain righteousness upon you.

Hosea 10:12

Therefore turn thou to thy God: keep mercy and judgment, and wait on thy God continually.

Hosea 12:6

Joel

And it shall come to pass afterward, that I will pour out my spirit upon all flesh; and your sons and your daughters shall prophesy, your old men shall dream dreams, your young men shall see visions:
Joel 2:28

The sun shall be turned into darkness, and the moon into blood, before the great and the terrible day of the LORD come.
Joel 2:31

And it shall come to pass, that whosoever shall call on the name of the LORD shall be delivered: for in mount Zion and in Jerusalem shall be deliverance, as the LORD hath said, and in the remnant whom the LORD shall call.
Joel 2:32

But let judgment run down as waters, and righteousness as a mighty stream.
Amos 5:24

Amos

And saviours shall come up on mount Zion to judge the mount of Esau; and the kingdom shall be the LORD's.
Obadiah 1:21

Obadiah

Jonah

I went down to the bottoms of the mountains; The earth with her bars was about me for ever: Yet hast thou brought up my life from corruption, O LORD my God. When my soul fainted within me I remembered the LORD: And my prayer came in unto thee, into thine holy temple. They that observe lying vanities forsake their own mercy. But I will sacrifice unto thee with the voice of thanksgiving; I will pay that that I have vowed. Salvation is of the LORD.

Jonah 2:6-9

Micah

But in the last days it shall come to pass, that the mountain of the house of the LORD shall be established in the top of the mountains, and it shall be exalted above the hills; and people shall flow unto it.
Micah 4:1

The LORD is good, a strong hold in the day of trouble; and he knoweth them that trust in him.
Nahum 1:7

Nahum

Habakkuk

The LORD God is my strength, And he will make my feet like hinds' feet,
And he will make me to walk upon mine high places...
Habakkuk 3:19

The LORD thy God in the midst of thee is mighty; he will save, he will rejoice over thee with joy; he will rest in his love, he will joy over thee with singing.
Zephaniah 3:17

Zephaniah

Thus saith the LORD of hosts; Consider your ways.
Haggai 1:7

Haggai

And the LORD shall be king over all the earth: in that day shall there be one LORD, and his name one.
Zechariah 14:9

Zechariah

Behold, I will send my messenger, and he shall prepare the way before me: and the Lord, whom ye seek, shall suddenly come to his temple, even the messenger of the covenant, whom ye delight in: behold, he shall come, saith the LORD of hosts.

Malachi 3:1

Malachi

Matthew

Blessed are the peacemakers: for they shall be called the children of God.
Matthew 5:9

Let your light so shine befor[e] men, that they may see you[r] good works, and glorify you[r] Father which is in heaven[.]
Matthew 5:1[6]

But seek ye first the kingdom of God, and his righteousness; and all these things shall be added unto you.
Matthew 6:33

Mark

For even the Son of man came not to be ministered unto, but to minister, and to give his life a ransom for many.
Mark 10:45

And when ye stand praying, forgive, if ye have ought against any: that your Father also which is in heaven may forgive you your trespasses.
Mark 11:25

And the angel answered and said unto her, The Holy Ghost shall come upon thee, and the power of the Highest shall overshadow thee: therefore also that holy thing which shall be born of thee shall be called the Son of God.
Luke 1:35

Luke

For with God nothing shall be impossible.
Luke 1:37

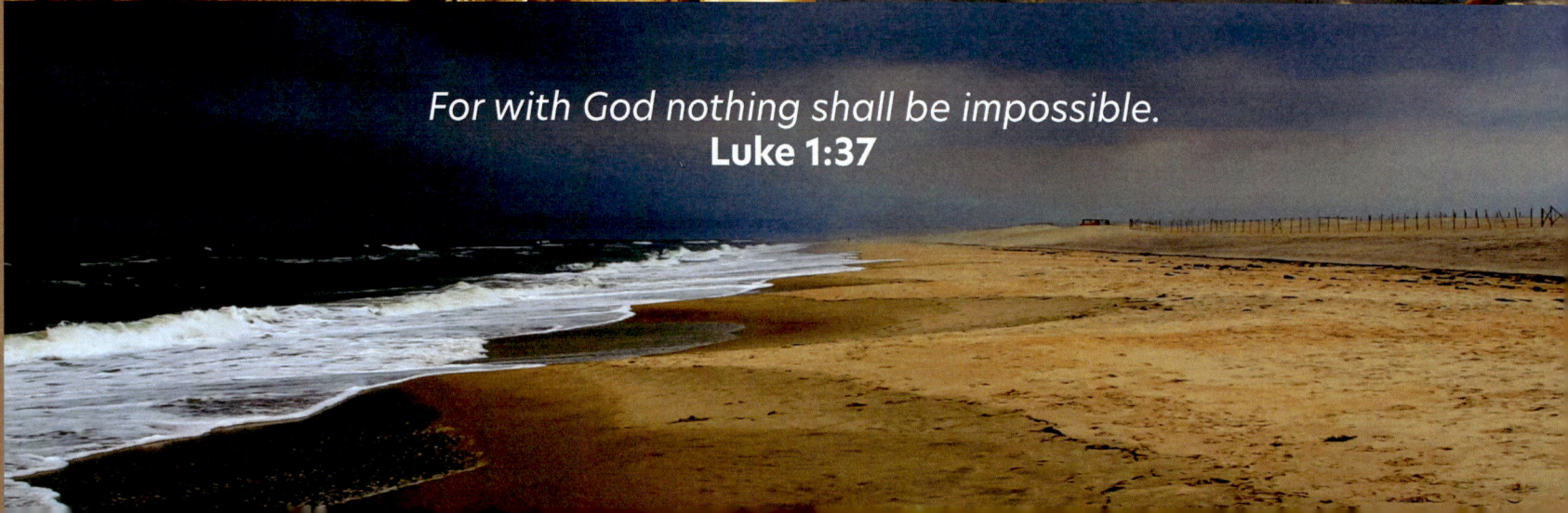

John

For God so loved the world, that he gave his only begotten Son, that whosoever believeth in him should not perish, but have everlasting life.
John 3:16

The thief cometh not, but for to steal, and to kill, and to destroy: I am come that they might have life, and that they might have it more abundantly.
John 10:10

A new commandment I give unto you, That ye love one another; as I have loved you, that ye also love one another.
John 13:34

Acts

Romans

For I reckon that the sufferings of this present time are not worthy to be compared with the glory which shall be revealed in us.
Romans 8:18

And we know that all things work together for good to them that love God, to them who are the called according to his purpose.
Romans 8:28

And be not conformed to this world: but be ye transformed by the renewing of your mind, that ye may prove what is that good, and acceptable, and perfect, will of God.
Romans 12:2

1 & 2 Corinthians

There hath no temptation taken you but such as is common to man: but God is faithful, who will not suffer you to be tempted above that ye are able; but will with the temptation also make a way to escape, that ye may be able to bear it.
1 Corinthians 10:13

And now abideth faith, hope, charity, these three; but the greatest of these is charity.
1 Corinthians 13:13

But we had the sentence of death in ourselves, that we should not trust in ourselves, but in God which raiseth the dead:
2 Corinthians 1:9

While we look not at the things which are seen, but at the things which are not seen: for the things which are seen are temporal; but the things which are not seen are eternal.
2 Corinthians 4:18

Galatians

I am crucified with Christ: nevertheless I live; yet not I, but Christ liveth in me: and the life which I now live in the flesh I live by the faith of the Son of God, who loved me, and gave himself for me.
Galatians 2:20

But the fruit of the Spirit is love, joy, peace, longsuffering, gentleness, goodness, faith, meekness, temperance: against such there is no law.
Galatians 5:22-23

For all the law is fulfilled in one word, even in this; Thou shalt love thy neighbour as thyself. But if ye bite and devour one another, take heed that ye be not consumed one of another. This I say then, Walk in the Spirit, and ye shall not fulfil the lust of the flesh. For the flesh lusteth against the Spirit, and the Spirit against the flesh: and these are contrary the one to the other: so that ye cannot do the things that ye would.
Galatians 5:14-17

Ephesians

For by grace are ye saved through faith; and that not of yourselves: it is the gift of God: not of works, lest any man should boast.
Ephesians 2:8-9

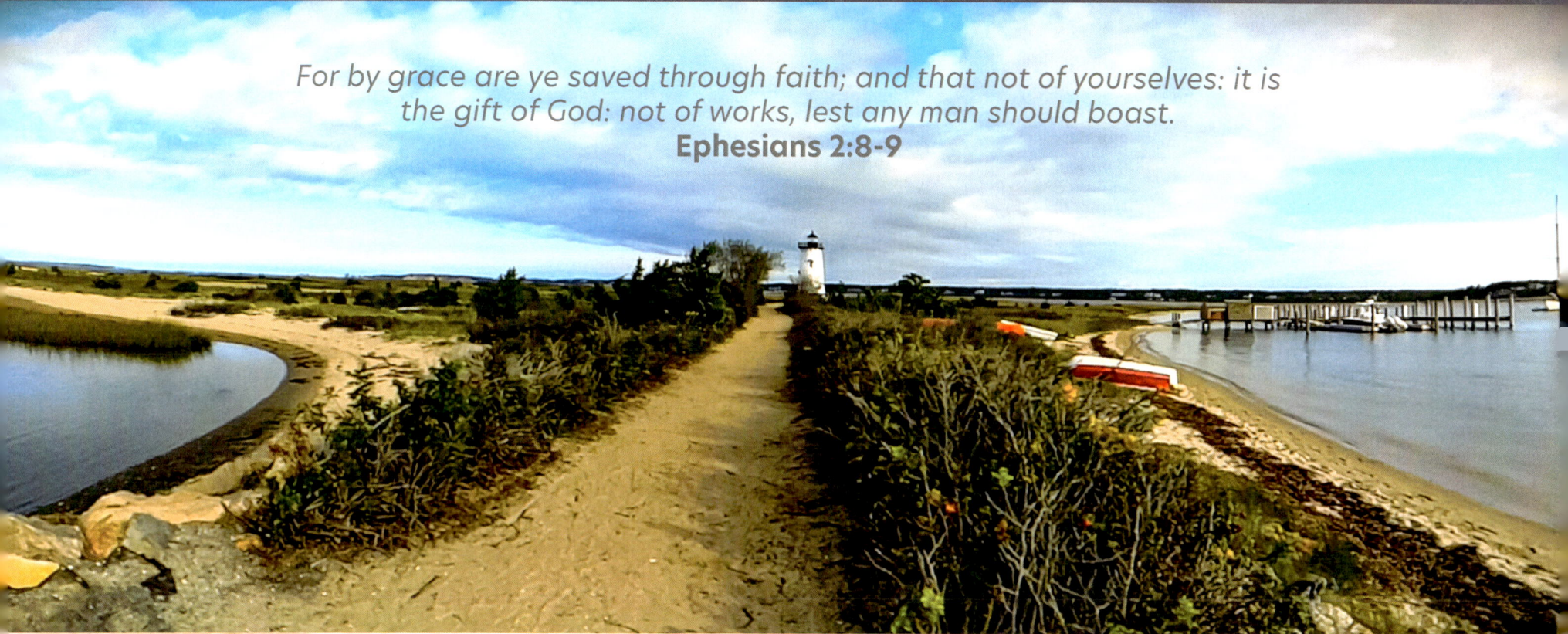

For we wrestle not against flesh and blood, but against principalities, against powers, against the rulers of the darkness of this world, against spiritual wickedness in high places.
Ephesians 6:12

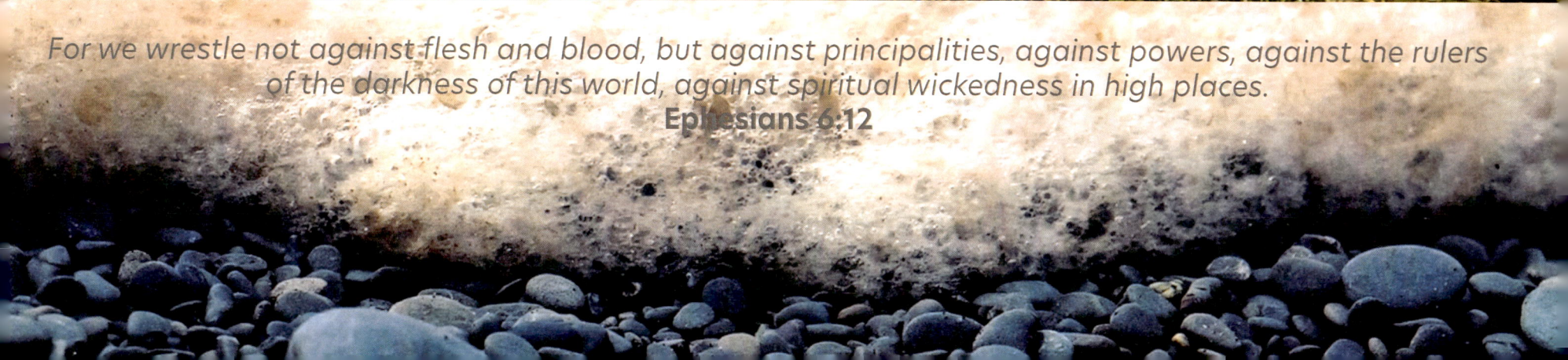

Philippians

Let nothing be done through strife or vainglory; but in lowliness of mind let each esteem other better than themselves.
Philippians 2:3

Do all things without murmurings and disputings: that ye may be blameless and harmless, the sons of God, without rebuke, in the midst of a crooked and perverse nation, among whom ye shine as lights in the world
Philippians 2:14-15

Finally, brethren, whatsoever things are true, whatsoever things are honest, whatsoever things are just, whatsoever things are pure, whatsoever things are lovely, whatsoever things are of good report; if there be any virtue, and if there be any praise, think on these things.
Philippians 4:8

I can do all things through Christ which strengtheneth me.
Philippians 4:13

Beware lest any man spoil you through philosophy and vain deceit, after the tradition of men, after the rudiments of the world, and not after Christ.
Colossians 2:8

And whatsoever ye do, do it heartily, as to the Lord, and not unto men
Colossians 3:23

Colossians

1 & 2 Thessalonians

For the Lord himself shall descend from heaven with a shout, with the voice of the archangel, and with the trump of God: and the dead in Christ shall rise first
I Thessalonians 4:16

Wherefore comfort yourselves together, and edify one another, even as also ye do.
I Thessalonians 5:11

See that none render evil for evil unto any man; but ever follow that which is good, both among yourselves, and to all men.
I Thessalonians 5:15

For the Lord himself shall descend from heaven with a shout, with the voice of the archangel, and with the trump of God: and the dead in Christ shall rise first
2 Thessalonians 1:3

Which is a manifest token of the righteous judgment of God, that ye may be counted worthy of the kingdom of God, for which ye also suffer
2 Thessalonians 1:5

God hath from the beginning chosen you to salvation through sanctification of the Spirit and belief of the truth
2 Thessalonians 2:13

1 & 2 Timothy

For there is one God, and one mediator between God and men, the man Christ Jesus
I Timothy 2:5

———

And without controversy great is the mystery of godliness: God was manifest in the flesh, justified in the Spirit, seen of angels, preached unto the Gentiles, believed on in the world, received up into glory.
I Timothy 3:16

———

Let no man despise thy youth; but be thou an example of the believers, in word, in conversation, in charity, in spirit, in faith, in purity.
I Timothy 4:12

For God hath not given us the spirit of fear; but of power, and of love, and of a sound mind.
2 Timothy 1:7

I have fought a good fight, I have finished my course, I have kept the faith
2 Timothy 4:7

Titus

In hope of eternal life, which God, that cannot lie, promised before the world began
Titus 1:2

I thank my God, making mention of thee always in my prayers
Philemon 1:4

Philemon

Hebrews

Let us hold fast the profession of our faith without wavering; (for he is faithful that promised;) and let us consider one another to provoke unto love and to good works: not forsaking the assembling of ourselves together, as the manner of some is; but exhorting one another: and so much the more, as ye see the day approaching.
Hebrews 10:23-25

James

Wherefore lay apart all filthiness and superfluity of naughtiness, and receive with meekness the engrafted word, which is able to save your souls.
James 1:21

But whoso looketh into the perfect law of liberty, and continueth therein, he being not a forgetful hearer, but a doer of the work, this man shall be blessed in his deed. If any man among you seem to be religious, and bridleth not his tongue, but deceiveth his own heart, this man's religion is vain.
James 1:25-26

Even so faith, if it hath not works, is dead, being alone.
James 2:17

The Lord is not slack concerning his promise, as some men count slackness; but is longsuffering to us-ward, not willing that any should perish, but that all should come to repentance.
2 Peter 3:9

But grow in grace, and in the knowledge of our Lord and Saviour Jesus Christ. To him be glory both now and for ever. Amen.
2 Peter 3:18

1 & 2 Peter

1 John

If we confess our sins, he is faithful and just to forgive us our sins, and to cleanse us from all unrighteousness.
1 John 1:9

2 John

And this is love, that we walk after his commandments. This is the commandment, That, as ye have heard from the beginning, ye should walk in it.
2 John 1:6

3 John

Beloved, I wish above all things that thou mayest prosper and be in health, even as thy soul prospereth.
3 John 1:2

Sunday Girl

Keep yourselves in the love of God, looking for the mercy of our Lord Jesus Christ unto eternal life.
Jude 1:21

Jude

And every creature which is in heaven, and on the earth, and under the earth, and such as are in the sea, and all that are in them, heard I saying, Blessing, and honour, and glory, and power, be unto him that sitteth upon the throne, and unto the Lamb for ever and ever.
Revelation 5:13

And I heard as it were the voice of a great multitude, and as the voice of many waters, and as the voice of mighty thunderings, saying, Alleluia: for the Lord God omnipotent reigneth. Let us be glad and rejoice, and give honour to him: for the marriage of the Lamb is come, and his wife hath made herself ready.
Revelation 19:6-7

And I John saw the holy city, new Jerusalem, coming down from God out of heaven, prepared as a bride adorned for her husband.
Revelation 21:2

And he that sat upon the throne said, Behold, I make all things new. And he said unto me, Write: for these words are true and faithful.
Revelation 21:5

Revelation

Through the light of the lens,
Capturing imprints in time,
These places and spaces,
Scattered across geographies and continents,
Places sometimes vast and spectacular,
Sometimes intimate and quaint,
Inspired me to share these images
That are all the work of my favorite artist,
The art of God.

This world is His canvas,
His love poured out on it
For our eyes to see
And our hearts to feel;
Each image a little window
into God's divine plan.

-Connie Henry

www.ingramcontent.com/pod-product-compliance
Ingram Content Group UK Ltd.
Pitfield, Milton Keynes, MK11 3LW, UK
UKRC031008100225
454903UK00001B/1